And The Angels Speak

Rebecca J. Steiger

Contents

Dedication

Douglas D. Brown
August 4, 1942 – November 8, 2010

I have known many wonderful people in my life. However, there is one that touched so many hearts and opened so many doors for others. That person was Douglas D. Brown, my brother, my friend and ordinary man who enjoyed life.

He had stage four cancer, which ate away his body but never his courage or his mind. He spent his life learning and studying all he could, about anything and everything he could find. He opened his mind to new and unknown possibilities. He took care of wild life management, but enjoyed the animals and birds in his backyard most of all. He hiked mountains all over the world. He skied, bicycled and enjoyed all that nature had to offer! He was a free spirit, yet so different from me.

After Doug's passing, the Angels brought him in to see me and he gave me this wonderful message. He was with my father, who passed away in November of 2007. I listened to his quiet voice as he spoke. He said, "I was walking uphill with no place to go except home to those I loved." He asked that we look after his wife, to let her be a part of our lives and that he will live on through her. He asked me to dedicate my life to continue to helping others who come to me. He understood my calling and everything was clear. He loved all of us in this family.

I must tell you, from my own personal experiences, you never die. Your physical form is left behind, but when the Angels come, you only change clothes and go home. You continue to live in a different form, in a different way. You will be cross the veil and live between two worlds, Heaven and Earth. Really, there is no difference you see, as Earth is an extension of Heaven.

So, I say goodbye to my brother and my friend, to Doug's life in the human form and look forward to seeing and hearing more from him in a spiritual way. Loving you always, my wonderful brother!

Foreword

I have known Rebecca for many years and many lifetimes. For a while, in the course of her journey, she had the proverbial bucket over her light. It took a tornado to blow her away the clutter and a love intervention. To bring her to understanding of her precious gifts and the she is meant to do. This book is a stepping stone for Rebecca on her way to becoming the radiant and abundant person that she is. In the writing of it she has brightened the path for all of us. Enjoy!

Mary Lou Ridge, ND, LMT +

Preface

Being the intuitive person that I am, I had always known that I was going to write a book. Entirely different from this one, it was going to tell everything about everyone I knew, more like a "soap opera" type of thing!

I traveled a lot back then, had lots of sex and smut stories on everybody I was around. However, to my surprise, Spirit picked me up out of my box, shook me up a little and dropped me to the ground. I started writing alright, about something I knew absolutely nothing about!

In 1993, I was in a tornado with my four-year-old grandson, who clung to my chest. We were blown out of a house, landing in a field under a satellite dish! During this time, I was either knocked out or blacked out and stood before God (the Supreme Being) and His judgment. My sister-in-law, who had previously passed on, was leaning over His shoulder and said; "Not now Lord; for she still has many things to do."

I went around, wondering what it was that I was supposed or meant to do. I was afraid that, at any time, God might decide that I was not doing things right and take me home. Now, I know. What I had thought was the worst and scariest thing that ever happened to me actually was the best! Giving me many gifts and blessings!

Shortly after the tornado, my grandson would talk about our Guardian Angels. "You know, he would say the ones we saw during the Tornado". I would agree with him and go on. Never realizing that he too could and did see Angels.

One day when I was driving with a friend down a gravel road, by the cemetery where my grandfather is buried, I suddenly saw this huge Angel standing in the middle of the road. His purple robe and giant wings were a sight to see. I asked him who he was; and he said "Cervihel", my Guardian Angel. Okay, now I was thinking first that "I have never heard of Cervihel" and second "Am I going totally crazy?"

When I got home, I called my neighbor, Patti; she had a lot of Angel books, and she couldn't find him in any of them. So, she finally went on the internet and looked him up. He, of course was there. Cervihel, is an Angel of strength! He helped David slay Goliath.

Now, I am thinking, "WOW"! I really have seen an Angel" …

Then, I started seeing Angels everywhere, literally all over the place, around other people, in the sky, trees, and fields. What a wonderful gift I was given!

One day, I was in the bathtub and the Angels blasted me with information, telling me things I'd never thought about before. Two hours later, I was able to get out of the bath. I started writing; and when I'd write, they'd talk faster. It really was hard, at times, to keep up. They had so much to tell me and they had waited until I was ready to receive this information.

Then, I not only discovered my Angels, but I could tell others who their Angels and guides are. Angels are giving me information about troubles in someone's life that had kept them from moving forward on their paths. I have never been wrong when I channel for others.

One day, when I was channeling for a girl, I had just met, I saw her deceased mother over her right shoulder. I described her mother to her. Sure enough, she appeared as when she was the happiest in her earthly life. She had a message for her daughter; and I gave the message to her. To my surprise, she knew exactly what it was! Then, the channel of crossing over was opened.

Someone asked me what I thought about meditation, that I should learn to meditate. I walked outside and saw a Rainbow; it was bright and beautiful. The next thing I knew, I was doing a guided meditation for others; helping keep the balance and giving them positive direction in their lives. All done by clearing my mind and asking the Angels to help. So now I not only meditate, but also do guided meditation to help others.

Ever since I was in the tornado, I had healing energy in my hands; and everyone would say, "Oh, so you do Reiki?" My answer was "No, I Don't." I knew what Reiki was; because my neighbor and friend Patti is a Reiki Master, and so is her sister Mary Lou.

Then I was working one day for a chiropractor and had a patient come in with some severe problems; and they called me to the back to an exam room to do some energy work on him. I did not know this man of many gifts was a Reiki Master. After he came to the window to pay his bill, he asked me how long I'd been doing Reiki. We then had a discussion and he (who is now a dear friend) gave me my Reiki I and II attunements. What a wonderful gift that was. Opening more channels of health for others! I also began to get more information for my clients as I worked on them. I could actually see what organs were blocked, where trouble was on their path, and so being able to be of more help to them and their healing process.

I still receive and heal others through Reiki; I firmly believe in the energy work. One day when Patti was doing Reiki on me, I received my master's attunement through Jesus. Who better to attune you! When I got off the table and told Patti of my experience, she agreed that now was the time for me to complete my master's. I am now a Reiki Master, using the energy every day to help others.

Well, I thought that I had opened all that there was to open. Wrong! I then started seeing the ascended masters and print in very small letters being filed into my mind. As crazy as this sounds, this book is the Angels' gift to you. Spirit sent me back to write this work, channeled from the Angels for you.

Acknowledgments

I want to thank many of those who gave me encouragement, love, and understanding.

A special thanks to Mary Lou Ridge, who has always been there and understood.

Pat Montgomery, who was the first one to share my Angel experience. Garry who accepted me as I am.

My two wonderful children, Amy and Andy, with whom I share my life.

Five wonderful grandchildren.
My parents, for who they are.
Steven, whose wisdom is great.

I wish to thank everyone I have ever met, good or bad, for my knowledge comes from all my life experiences. I thank you all for sharing my experiences on this path of life.

A special thanks to those who saw me as a sane person, not as one who had totally lost it, when my journey truly began. Their understanding and patience helped to heal me and gave me concrete evidence that there is a much larger force that surrounds us!

I thank you!

Rebecca's Metaphysical Moment

I am your heart, I am your mind, I am your vision and your light
to follow.
This can be your life.

CHAPTER ONE
How You Perceive Yourself

May 16, 2003

How others perceive you is unimportant! It's how you perceive yourself that matters. Humanity is in for the big "let down" of one another.

When I first wrote this book, the Angels told me that "the bombing has just started" and that much more was to come worldwide. How right they were. We have been hit hard by terrorists who have created diversions. New terrorist groups have appeared. Don't be afraid but also don't let your guard down. This is a world cleansing. Many good ones will go; God is not happy with things right now and is sending His wrath in many different ways. Drought, hunger, storms, high seas; mountains will crumble and fall; oceans will rise with fury. We have turned our backs on God and what he intended for us.

We live in fear of death and destruction. So, we have called in, we have created our own destruction. This will last for 50 years and then a clearing will come; worldwide peace will prevail. No nuclear war at this time - hopefully not later. The powers will see.

The Spirits are gathering for those who commit suicide. Many will stay to see the life and errors we have created upon this Earth and universe. We must repair the Earth and universe in order to live upon it for a thousand more years. The end of this time is near; but another better time on this Earth will take place.

The veil is opening for those who are willing simply to walk through it, to see the other side and what humanity must do to save this Earth and universe. Going back to the old way and caring for the Earth is not a bad way to start. Getting rid of chemicals and pollution, not only of the Earth and universe but also of humanities, minds and bodies. It will prolong the life of one-self. Live in the now and knowing. You are here to direct yourself and others to the now, the knowing you create. Some are behind and some ahead. Travel the universe and the Earth, to help others in need and trouble. Your abundance will come in many ways, some strange to you. Keep the flow of abundance coming and always accept it with love.

Some are on their path; and know who they are. Others judge too harshly, but they cannot be successful by going in that direction. We judge ourselves more than we do others.

By successfully healing the body, you heal the mind through Spirit. You have to be more flexible for those around you who do not always understand. They are in a forest and have not come out. They fear the ones they need to help; but helping themselves is the first step. So do not focus on the when; for, they will come to their own greatness in time, depending on their path choices. They can prolong it or have it sooner; it is their choice. They cling to a cliff, but do not need to.

Remember, things never end; they just keep turning like the wheels on a wagon. You are above reproach when you talk to Spirit more. Have great compassion for all living things. Remember to focus for a little while every day.

Then you will heal all things and have compassion for all things on this Earth. Those who choose to live, they will receive God's gifts.

Use them wisely. They have brought you this far and will carry you much farther, as you grow.

Touch the Earth and heal the ground (it's like a morning hug), and to ground yourself. You can fly with the Angels and travel through space to places unknown to man. Always let Spirit guide you to those things that need your love, attention and healing; living in the present moment, by going back to the old way of life.

You generate your own fear and distrust of others who cling to you; let this go. You have been given energy enough for all. You are not tired, merely lazy, fearing the man who tells you all is wrong! Forcing you out is not a problem; you always have what you need to grow.

You will then give yourself to no one and everyone. The powers that be know what is happening; but they cannot stop the terrorist who will be found on their journey to Cuba! Their strength still continues and will continue; without them, new even more dangerous and corrupt men will come and try to take over! Watch them slither by in the dark, the darkness of people's minds, playing on their fears and hungering for more knowledge and a place to hide. People cannot hide from the unjust world. They can only fight it with love and healing, expanding their conscious minds and spirits, lifting all humanity up and proceeding forward into life by stepping into the light. For, your job is here and at hand. Expand yourself and your direction becomes clearer and more intense.

Rebecca's Metaphysical Moment

God created the Heaven's and the Earth, then He created you to
enjoy this heavenly life.

CHAPTER TWO

The Creation of You

June, 2003

The light years are coming, awaking the soul and connecting you to God, healing all of those around you. Your physical being becomes brighter, night turns into day for you. You will shine like the moon and stars and become a heavenly being. For you see, you are already a heavenly being. You were created by God through your parents and dropped to Earth by Spirit. The human connection is what changed your light into darkness.

Your mind is the most powerful thing you possess. It processes your thoughts, making the commands on the nerves and muscles in the body. It creates the way you move and the way you react to a certain situation, all taught to you by man.

You let go of God's will because you've been trained by man to react and think as man, not as God intended. You have become attached to material things and not the spiritual things as God provided here on Earth. We only use half of our brains, not allowing the other half to be seen or to work. This then strains the heart and creates illness in the body. You become fearful, creating the illness. If for only a few minutes a day you allow the right side of your brain to function, it will open the heart charka and allow the light of love to flow in and create a new experience called love, to enter the body and start the healing process through love and Spirit of God. You must first heal the mind and be open to receive the healing of the body.

Run a mental picture, visualizing bright white light healing the mind and the body. Bring it through the crown chakra, down through the body and out your feet and hands. If you tell yourself, you are healing and healed, then you will be. Relieve the stress your mind has created and transferred into the body, then your problems will melt away and you will start seeing things clearer. Colors become brighter and clearer and joy will replace your stress.

Stirring the mind up is a good thing and makes you feel alive. Because guess what? You are alive and your thoughts belong to only you! Your mind should only be controlled by you. Man can take away everything you have, but he cannot take your thoughts away! God gave you your mind, not man, so turn your brain around and communicate to God by using the right side of your brain occasionally and see how the left side starts sending different signals to the body and all things and people around you. This is your gift from God the spirit maker. Man is the spirit taker, hollowing out our minds, taking away our spirit and filling our minds with greed, stress and sickness. Man creates our thinking process to follow him and not God, manipulating our minds to fear God and all good things, creating illness for man's profit. When we have the knowledge, you need to create good health within yourself and a loving connection to all things through God, as your god spirit intended! All by using the other half of your brain and few minutes a day, keeping the connection to God going and growing, allowing the light of all things to be reflected through you.

Then you will shine through the darkness of night, on through the darkness of day. All things are possible through God's love and your mind! Growing through spirit is truly connecting the mind, the body and the spirit to all things. Through God's love and our minds, we can create a new world filled with peace around the world by tearing down the false idols of man. By listening to our god spirit and by see who we really are, not who man says we are. Watch out for the false prophets, look through them and into their souls and you will find darkness, fear and smallness of the world. Make your world larger by sending love and healing into the world by walking past the false prophet, by overturning evil through love and by connecting your spirit with God's spirit. Becoming open to all thoughts you create in your mind. You will never be wrong when you stand in the light. Share this heavenly place called life in human form with others through your spirit consciousness with

Godly things provided through your Godly spirit. Standing in your own light, the false profit has no light and will disappear in your light. What a powerful being you truly are!

By exfoliating the dead cells in the brain, you have created new and more powerful brain cells to guide you along your path. You have created a brilliance within your own being. When you do this, others will look at you differently and follow you! Let your heart lead you and your head propel in all that you do.

Rebecca's Metaphysical Moment

Be aware of all things that surround you in this life by opening the mind and the heart.

CHAPTER THREE
Opening the Mind and Heart

October 09, 2003

Now is the time for people to open their minds and their hearts to all possibilities, to change their thinking, to open their worlds by doing what is necessary in this life's truest form; listening to their inner selves, the Spirit connection. You can never be wrong by doing this. The gut or root chakra speaks out, the heart speaks out and the head speaks out in unison. Bring the answers through your Spirit connection and not man. We live this moment for today, not tomorrow or yesterday. Live in the moment of truth and when you experience even one moment of truth today, right now, you will change your life forever. You will see that all things change and light will appear, even if you only see the light for a few minutes today and feel the joy and peace it brings you. You then will continue to search and touch the light tomorrow! What a wonderful gift Spirit has given us, here on Earth, to reach beyond ourselves to God through a small space as large as the universe, through a speck of light, changing our courses in life, giving us hope for the moment and the future, carrying us to a higher plane, a higher concept, changing our thinking patterns, eliminating our fears of unknown, and making us intervals of time and space, where there is no time!

Time is a manmade illusion. Light is a spectrum of being, a guide to the inner self, to the other side of our thinking, our being. Now we can truly know our spirit selves in human form. Then, everything will start changing because the way you see things then will change and the healing of one's self will begin. Some things will lose their importance; others will start manifesting into a larger more positive thing. So, open the chakras and allow the thought process to change. Your prayers are then answered, getting rid of fear and self-doubt, knowing the positive side of life, getting rid of your "I CAN'T" negative side. Allow the abundance of Spirit being in you to surround and protect you, giving you the knowledge and power you truly deserve, creating a powerful person who is connected to the Earth and universe as we all should be.

Nothing is scary when the lights are on and allowing you to see. Only darkness holds the unseen fear.

By standing in light consciousness and surrounding yourself with light, you will create a new and different world. So, if for only a few moments, clear your mind and focus on nothing. By focusing on yourself and letting the thoughts, pictures and colors flow, you will be told the answers you seek. Do not fear the truth; embrace it and celebrate the solutions in you and your life. A changing of the light force within you opens you to a realm of the possible. It can change your work status and marriage status, bringing you more love and abundance. But we have to love and accept who we are first. We have to be filled with the positive, letting go of the negative and charging our batteries while being human and accepting God and His presence; the God within us, whoever that may be. He is knocking at your door; please, won't you answer His call and open the door to expanding and prolonging your life, becoming joyful, happy and at peace with all things on this Earth.

Do we not see God in all shapes and sizes? We all come in different shapes and sizes. Do we not strive in our own ways to be perfect and pleasing when, in reality, we already are all perfect because God made us all that way? When you take a wrong turn off the freeway, do you not take the twists and turns to get you back on the freeway? So why stay lost in life when all you have to do is turn around and go back to the freeway of life? Simple? Yes, the simple things you can do is to accept who you are, who you can be and to find the spirit inside you. How? Remember to focus and listen to the inner you, traveling through time and space, moving you forward to a more positive and productive way of doing things, all done with the heart, mind and spirit connection.

The preacher says, "Don't you want to be on the BUS"!? I say "hell, no!" I want to drive my own bus. I want to own, if nothing else, my own life, my own mind and my own heart. Then I am truly led to God in the spirit of consciousness and love!

The closest thing to "new" we will ever have been our own body. Each day we have new blood, cells, skin, hair, nails and thoughts. We are new and whole every second of every day.

Rebecca's Metaphysical Moment

Building a bridge in your life is like stretching over and touching the other side of you.

CHAPTER FOUR

Have We Been Denied the Opportunity to Know Spirit?

September 09,2003

God is waiting for us to see the miracles which occur around us every day. The miracle of birth, the miracle of using our minds freely, the miracle of beauty seen in flowers, the miracle of life. Yet, do we see these things as miracles and gifts from God? No, not most of the time. Why? Because we take it all for granted. We don't think about how our lives would be without all the small miracles we receive every day. We're like Lott's wife, waiting to turn into a pillar of salt. Why? Because we cannot see; we are trained not to see. Man tells us what is good or bad; what miracles we can see and feel. Man tells us that we of little faith and knowledge cannot see.

We do not see miracles when they happen all around us every day. God sends messages to us every day. Can we see them, or hear them? No, because we do open our hearts or have faith enough in ourselves to see these things! We are not conscious of our surroundings, our energy or the energy of others. We simply have no faith! We have faith and fear combined. We still cannot see the miracles around us such as friends, family or reaching within ourselves for the love of a neighbor.

The boat of reality has drifted too far from the shore and there are not safety nets or tethers. Bull! The only safety net we have is in and through God's love and protection. Oh, but you say man will "protect me and prepare me to meet God and the celestial being." Well, think again. Man cannot prepare you; you have to prepare yourself. God has already forgiven your so called sins; when will you? Choose not man, but Spirit; the only one who counts. Spirit gives life or takes it away and creates the miracles that surround us. Spirit is the only one who loves us unconditionally. All we have to do is share our hearts with him and others. All we have to do is say in our hearts, "Thank You' or "I love you, God Spirit". That is all we have to do to lift our burdens, feel joy and fulfillment and to start healing our bodies, minds and spirits.

Listen to the miracle of a small singing bird. Oh, what a joy and beauty that surrounds that small creature; for, he sings the message of love from the universe of Spirit to you.

Receive the gift, it is freely given to you!

Day to day pressures can melt away the daily guidance from Spirit. Focus on your intent and celebrate your solutions. Most of all, join in on life and living. This is truly you land and your life; all is given to you as your playground; all is given freely to you through God. Through Spirit, all chores become joy, all sorrow becomes peace. Focus within and have faith that God Spirit hears all and returns all to us every day, creating simpler miracles for us to enjoy. And know that God too is inside and connected to each and every one of us.

The soul never dies! We are joined together in our spiritual bodies after this life; in the body of heavenly beings!

Rebecca's Metaphysical Moment

By opening the heart chakra and allowing the flow of love to come in, you will feel all the love that surrounds you

CHAPTER FIVE
Channel of Love

January 06, 2004

A channel of love surrounds us, even through the death of a loved one such as a family member. By opening our channels, we can receive the abundance of love. When someone dies, everyone is weeping tears of sorrow. They have not opened their channels of love. Even though their loved one has crossed over, their spirit can still be seen and touched when the channel of love is open.

Opening the consciousness and allowing yourself to truly feel is not loss, it's love. This will go on throughout our lives. This is felt through the spirit and the heart. Our lines of true communication are always open, all we have to do is to be willing to receive them. By not putting limits on or building walls around ourselves, we then become truly free and are not tangled in a web of fear. We will always feel a sense of loss for the physical form, but can always communicate with the spiritual form of never-ending life.

Focus on who is gone and with whom you want to communicate. Call them (just like a long-distance phone call) and have that conservation with them through love and the spiritual guidance through your Angels. It will fill your heart with so much love. Understanding yourself is the key. Take action and open your mind, you can truly become the powerful person you were meant to be. This is not a trick. This is only being open to receive the message of a loved one who has gone home ahead of us. What a wonderful gift has been provided for us!

I have dealt with many women who have the faces of Angels and the hearts of snakes. I had one involved in the dark arts, one who had an incestuous affair and one who was a party girl going from man to man. Remember, you cannot serve two masters, only one! We make life into hell on this heavenly Earth. That is not for which it was intended. Through my working with them in a loving and positive way, they have now rededicated their lives to learning and excepting Spirit's love and casting out the demons of the mind. Our thoughts sometimes can control us, instead of us controlling them.

Then, we are totally out of control. The flesh follows the mind. Interesting? You bet it is. Remember, God hears your thoughts 24 hours a day, just as if you were talking or praying to him. So, before you think a bad thought, stop and reprogram your mind.

When a troubled thought comes into your mind and surface problems arise, STOP! Focus for a minute or two, and turn those problems over to God and the Angels. Feel how much lighter you are, and how your problem will disappear. No struggle. Only Spirit knows what is best for us, not man. You are not rebelling against man, only following your Spiritual purpose. Open yourself, receive the true gifts from God and find purpose in life. You will be surprised at how much healthier you will become and problem-free too, because Spirit has taken those problems and released them as it should be.

Now, I am like a bulldog, who won't let go when I should. I can shake it to death, and finally when I am worn out, I then turn it over to the Angels who rapidly dissolve the problem. Why? Because I don't like problems. We manifest what we get and there are times when we manifest problems. It gives us excuses and there are no excuses. It keeps us in the box or the boat and we never get out. But we have lots of friends (who also are troubled) and we have lots of advice or sympathy, which feeds us and all those in the boat with you. Does it not make you feel better, more worthy or loved? BULL! It keeps us from coming to the light and finding our true selves, our purpose! So, POO on that. Take charge of your life and your destiny, fulfill your dreams and change the way you think. Accept Spirit and the Angelic realm. Become a whole person, the powerful person you were meant to be, simply by opening the consciousness!

We are put here to learn. We only learn by lessons taught to us, and every one we meet either brings us a gift or teaches us a lesson. Look for those things. Be open to receiving them graciously. In turn, you will always give them the gift of love. At that point, you literally have turned the tide and have healed deeper wounds within yourself.

Rebecca's Metaphysical Moment

Cutting the cords releases us from the box, showing us there is a better way.

CHAPTER SIX

Don't Be a Jack in the Box

July, 2004

Are you the type of person who needs someone to wind you up, for you to get out of your box? And then you let them pull your strings until it's time for them to put you back in the box? All the time you are so happy to do as they tell you to do, because you know that you are the perfect person, husband, wife, employee. All of that is great, but who are you? What are your dreams? Your destiny? So you think that's it. It's not easy, but that's it. I'll take care of myself later. I'll do something different later. I have to this for them now!

Well, let me tell you this one thing… You do not have to do anything.

Is stress killing you? Yes! But you are killing yourself. Are you truly caring and loving yourself? Can you stand in front of a mirror and say "I Love Me. I love who I am, and I love how I look. I love what I do?" If you cannot do this, then how can you truly love anyone or anything else? Do you love God or Spirit (or whatever name you choose for the Supreme Being)? Or do you spend your life fearing God or Spirit? Do you pray every day? Well, the answer is yes; you do pray every day. We all do for God or Spirit. He hears every thought and every word you think and say and knows every thought and word you have ever said.

We talk to our God all the time. So, now how does this change your thoughts and words? OOPS! Didn't know this, did you?

Man says you should fear God and do right or God will punish you for being you, for being different. Wrong! By loving God and truly opening the God self within you, you are filled with peace and love, standing in the golden light of healing. It is like standing in a meadow filled with sunlight and flowers, receiving true peace and abundance which surrounds us all. We are here today to show you how to achieve and feel the true love of Spirit! I am going to open your channel to God and the Angelic realm. This will make all things possible, even loving yourself as you are, completing and fulfilling your destiny, opening your path, answering your questions, freeing you from the Jack-In-The-Box!

First, let me tell you that God or Spirit is in each and every one of us. Look at the person next to you and you can see God! Look at this Earth, an extension of Heaven and you will see a heavenly place!

Look in the mirror and you will truly see a miracle made in God's image, doing God's work. We will teach you how to play, live, laugh and love. We are here to learn, to receive gifts from others around us.

So we are going to give you the opportunity to open your consciousness and pull you out of the past to walk into the light of a bright and new future! The choice is yours.

Everyone we meet brings us either a lesson or a gift. Learn from the lesson and receive the gifts gracefully. When we open the box, we then start the healing process of the mind, body and spirit. We then can embrace life and feel the peace and joy of each day. Fear and dread will disappear! Mundane tasks become fun. We then will change only existing in this life to truly living life.

Remember, you cannot serve two masters! Only one! The choice is yours. The only choice is the Spirit of God! Not man's laws, but God's all-loving laws. And yes, there are rules to follow, a schedule to keep and a bus to catch!

Join us on the ride to glory, filling your life with the unexpected love, light, peace, and joy, healing it will bring.

Now, let me tell you about my awakening and meeting God, standing before Him and having my life reviewed in the Supreme presence; the tornado, my connection with the Angels, my miracle, my rebirth, my knowing that all things are possible and that all small things are great!

Heaven is here, and it does surround us! There are no "have to's", only choices! And the choice is yours to live a fuller, easier, and more complete life through the love of Spirit. Move forward out of the darkness and into the light of Jesus Christ. Your days will be filled with expectation and wonder of all things upon this Earth, quieting the mind and listening to God, hearing the wonders of the universe, starting life anew each day and throwing away the clocks; we have all the time in the world and then some. Become energized, we have all the energy of the universe at our disposal.

Healing and combining the mind, body and spirit, seeing that everything you have ever done in your life has brought you here. There are no wrong, only wrong turns that teach us the lessons of living. Be thankful for the wrongs and the lessons. Celebrate the solutions! I will show you how simple and fun life can become when you open the consciousness. Colors will be brighter when you open the consciousness. Smiles will replace frowns and troubles will simply be another lesson, enabling us to receive a gift at the end. How is all of this possible? By simply letting go and connecting with God through love, not force, but love by opening the consciousness and connecting the heart and the mind simply by feeling and knowing your spirit self! All of the answers to your questions of life are within you. For, you are a powerful being and able to create the life you were truly meant to live, the person you are truly put on this heavenly Earth to be.

I am a seer! I see things that have blocked a person's past and have kept them from the future! I see God and the Angels. I see the wonders and the troubles of life. I am here to lead and serve all things upon this Earth. What a great and wonderful privilege and what a wonderful gift I have been given. You too have gifts. What are they?

After today, I hope you will find your gifts and open your gifts from God! The choice is yours. I can only show you how, you have to do the work in order to receive the gift. The choice is yours. Except for the gift, standing in the glory of Spirit. All things are possible, creating balance, abundance and feeling love of our Supreme creator while using the ancient wisdom of the Angels to help guide us. They love to be used, for that is their purpose. See the humor in one's life, laugh and rejoice with the Angels.

Laughter is one of our most precious gifts, healing and completing us. It frees the spirit and lets it soar. Laughter is infectious. When you smile within, you radiate instantly a wonderful light energy that affects all things around you. Life becomes easier, colors are brighter and people are warmer, drawing not only you into the light but also those around you. You not only heal yourself, but also others. Open a channel of loving energy, taking you to the mount with Jesus. This brings you to a higher self-awareness, opening you to experience the emotion of true love while respecting yourself and taking care of your body and healing your body, making you more conscious of the energy that surrounds you.

You will feed the thoughts of love to others by feeding the thoughts of love to yourself.

Rebecca's Metaphysical Moment

We are all made of the same ingredients. How you use them is what you become.

CHAPTER SEVEN
How to Make a Meatloaf

August 16, 2004

Hamburger, onion, egg, tomato sauce, something to hold it all together; cook at 325 for one hour.

Everyone has the same recipe and all of the ingredients can be bought, but putting the ingredients together is the hardest part! Wouldn't you agree? Making a meatloaf also takes time, it takes willingness to try. It's made from love. The perfect ingredients, the perfect pan, all of it goes together. Is it the same with life? Do you work to make your space, your life perfect, just right? So you follow man's laws and ride the fear of living? Do you venture into the unknown and reach inside your God-self for the answers, or do you let man tell you all that you need to know? If you do, you are wrong! Man can only tell you what he knows and who he is, not who you are, not what you know, not even what you believe! Only Spirit knows!

You were sent to this Earth, this beautiful extension of Heaven, a place we call home, to learn, to give and receive from others! Have you found your home here? Have you truly enjoyed the home you live in? Do you find peace of mind, enjoyment? A house is a shelter, a roof over your head designed to do what? To keep you safe, warm, dry and so-forth! Your true home can be anywhere when the body, the mind and the spirit are aligned and as one. You can only live within what God has made for us, what gifts he has given us. Yet, you fear Him! But it is such a loving eternity. He is the father, mother and child that is within all of us. Put the ingredients together, mix it well, and let it cook until done, then see what you have become!

You will have no fear. You will become more alive through love, not only of yourself but for others as well. We are an extension of the heavenly body. We make our lives Heaven or hell. We create the image through the mind, our thoughts and words, hate and fear. Then, life can become hell. Change the above and life becomes Heaven.

When you feel challenged, when the lesson is given, look for and receive the gift! Don't try to fix it before it breaks! One small piece is a whole by itself. It's all in how you view it. Cut the ties that weigh you down and allow yourself to fly! Break the bonds and forces that keep us in fear and hatred. Keep close to your heart the love of yourself! We all deserve better from ourselves. We all deserve to love ourselves, because we have all the time in the world. We can do whatever we choose in our own time, not in man's. Throw away what does not belong in your world! For, we all create our own world! It's amazing to me that we create our own world yet so many cannot live in the world that they've created! Well, if you can't, you have all the time in the world to change yours and to redirect your energies. Focus and change your world that feels so uncomfortable to live in by using your God given ingredients of the mind, body and spirit. Give up debilitating things like fear, hate and depression. You will literally heal yourself and become a true child of Spirit! You then will be whole and molded by yourself, ready to bake to become the perfect person you were meant to be!

I suggest you hug yourself and at least one other person daily. Turn frowns into smiles, trials into triumphs. Plant seeds for growth and harvest regularly! Dance with yourself, sing with the Angels and feel life! Feel the true power of Spirit! You will literally increase your energy 100%, and then some. Everything you need to make a fabulously perfect meatloaf has been given to you FREE of charge! Bon Appetite!

Here are a few suggestions for a happier you:

- List things that make you happy! (Do more of these.)
- List things that make you unhappy! (Get rid of these.)
- Write about the most favorite time in your life!
- Think about your absolute most favorite time!
- List your favorite foods.
- Think about your favorite person! (Spend more time with him or her.)
- List your favorite music! (Listen to it more often.)

Rebecca's Metaphysical Moment

Sometimes life and the mind are too quiet. We need to lift the veil of depression and silence to let the light shine through and make some noise.

Follow the sun and let the Angels guide you through inner thought.

CHAPTER EIGHT
The Mind Can Play Funny Tricks

December 01,2003

One minute, you're up high and happy, feeling great. The next minute, the mind flips, all is gone and depression sets in like a stone. Why? Because our thought processes allows it. We let ourselves become down and depressed. Our energy literally sags. Why? Because we expect to be successful in life, living up to everyone's expectations when really, we have everything, we need to take care of our minds and bodies. We overload our minds and get caught up in keeping up with what is projected to be our lives. What we see in movies and on television is how we think we are supposed to live. How Wrong! Pretty woman gets prince charming and prince charming turns into a Frog!

We are always looking for our true purpose in life, out and around us all of the time; whether consciously or subconsciously. We are out there looking when what we need to do is communicate with ourselves, get in touch with nature (our gift from mother Earth) look above to Spirit who surrounds us and see that our purpose is what we are now. Quit storing the "what if's", live in this moment and do what is right for you. You are unique in your own way. When life gives you lemons, celebrate the gift and make lemonade. Accept God's presence and use your mind to focus on the love that surrounds you, making the mind work for your greatness. The now; not an illusion of what man says you are, but who you are, surrounding you with abundance of life, filling you with love and greatness. Remember, you are a powerful being. If you're centered and grounded, you then can fly and reach inside yourself through meditation and be the powerful being you truly are.

Have you ever tried just being? Not taking on more responsibility, not judging someone else, not expecting someone to do something (this is a form of judging), not disliking someone or something. Most people live about the same way. DON'T! It is life-destroying. You have to change it to "I don't like their ways". Remember, they too are one their own paths and they too are out there looking for their passion in life, and who they truly are.

We are all hunters. Each one of us is looking for happiness, greatness, life, a soul mate, job, peace, etc. Hunters have to be very quiet and listen for the life-hunting answers, else they leave empty handed. Learn from this, listen to your inner self and let the heart lead you and the mind propel you!

Accept! Accept all that you are and all that you can be in this life on this heavenly playground. Don't limit yourself. All things are possible. Now is the time to become aware of one's self, to start the changes of the mind in yourself; respect and love yourself in the unique form you are. See others with respect of who and what they are, no matter what. Visit yourself and who you are. By getting in touch with the true you, the real you, you will learn more about this person and the role you are to play in this life.

The adventure is wonderful and the purity of the Godlike person you are will unfold and emerge like the wings of a butterfly. What a magnificent sight to behold; a true miracle of life.

Rebecca's Metaphysical Moment

Stretch your creative side, use your imagination and create the life you want.

CHAPTER NINE
Conscious Reality

June,2005

Conscious reality is not do something we have to chase after, because then we are chasing unreality! Conscious reality does not hide from us. We hide so well from ourselves!

We, as humans, are afraid to look within ourselves. Why? Because no one has told us we can do this. What we've been told or programmed to do is to listen to others (the man). That is when we listen to ourselves. What will you see? What mistakes will we make, what wrong decisions? Don't we do this every day? We do this by not opening to one's self, by fearing ourselves, by trying to do the unnatural thing and by trying to do what someone to whom we give our power tells us to do.

Trust yourself and open your heart. Turn off the television, put down the smartphone and block the outside noise that clutters your life. This is when you will find true peace within.

Trust yourself to live out your reality, not someone who is not you. They only see you as they want to. Or, perhaps, they don't see you at all. You need to take control of your own reality and become the powerful and great person that you were meant to be!

There is no shifting of life roles, only an awaking of the spirit to see the reality. Mistakes will be made. However, you will understand the lessons and be able to receive the gifts by understanding of why the mistakes were made!

Confusing? No, absolutely not! But the good news is that you have gained control of your destiny, your reality and your life without judgments or fear! You become more positive in the things you do, gaining confidence and the ability to make decisions about your life while bringing joy to your soul and healing the mind and body by opening the spirit source you have within you. This literally propels you towards a different kind of life, liking yourself and those around you, making you whole, complete and one with God.

We fear birth and death. We fear living because we do not trust in our Lord God. We only trust the man who tells us about God, but we do not trust ourselves enough to see our Godlike selves and really touch the spirit of ourselves! Through prayer and meditation, we hold the light. This heals us mentally, physically and spiritually. When you clear your own path, laughter and happiness will surround you and you will bring others to the light, through your light.

Rebecca's Metaphysical Moment

When we pray, we are talking to God. When we meditate, we open the door for God to talk to us.

CHAPTER TEN

Meditation: The Purest Form of Prayer

2005

Through meditation, we combine the body, mind and spirit. By clearing the mind, we create a beautiful and wonderful experience! We relax, going deeper inside ourselves and discovering a channel to the soul. We release stress and toxic negative energy, replacing these things with love through the heart and filling us with joy and wonderment. This surrounds us with the healing light while we experience true peace, living in the moment and joining and opening ourselves to God's presence. We now have a totally new experience. We have no fear and no anger. We have a feeling of self-love and completeness through God's love! We know, at that moment, that we are never alone. We are part of Spirit and Spirit is in each and every one of us.

We know that we do nothing wrong, that everything and every experience we have ever had, good or bad, has led us to this point. We know to accept ourselves and to accept changes that we need to make, but the choice of course is ours. We know that God is real and lives in each of us, although we all see God differently! But what is important, after knowing this, is what do we need to do with that knowledge? Nothing!

If we take a few minutes each day to clear the spaces in our minds, God's presence will become clearer to us. Through meditation, we can speak directly and clearly to God, receiving the answers we need to maintain our physical, mental and spiritual well-being. God gives us knowledge, power and freedom to ask any question at any given moment and the freedom to receive the information we need at any given time. What a wonderful gift! When a gift becomes reality, it then becomes truth and the truth is what truly sets us free! Then, we have someone with whom to share our experiences and someone who will not judge our actions. We will see the truth in all things to help in times of stress, anger, grief and sickness. We are never truly alone! We do have someone to show us our path and a better way and we simply do this through meditation. This is when we can let go of fear, stress, sickness, anger and grief; the list goes on. We then can feel the healing and changing within ourselves and see the powerful beings that we truly are.

All you have to do is enjoy the process through your self-discovery.

Meditation is the direct link to your God-source.

Remember that it is not what form of meditation you do, it's just that you do meditate! Reach within yourself and touch your God Spirit, through the purest form of prayer. "Don't Break the Connection"!

Rebecca's Metaphysical Moment

Does negativity have your life turned upside down? Learn to flip the coin, turn the negative into positive.

CHAPTER ELEVEN
Turning Negative Energy Into Positive

July,2005

We receive negative energy a number of ways! Sometimes, it is purposely sent our way by someone who is mad at us or by someone who means us harm, intentional harm. Other times, we receive it from people who are just negative that we happen to be around, either by choice or not. Jealousy is also a very powerful and intentional way of sending negative, dark energy! We must understand that there are those who are around us who do not stand in the light of positive living and thinking. Be aware of the energies around you! We all meet people with whom we are uncomfortable. We go someplace and it doesn't feel right. Well, it's the negative energy that we feel which gives us that uneasy feeling.

People can develop all sorts of illnesses because of the negative energy they pick up around them, including heart problems, cancer and stroke. People sometimes die suddenly! Remember, the negative energy will attach to the weakest organ, the one that is the most exposed and vulnerable. I know, most people are not aware of the energies around them. However, you are aware of illness when you don't feel well, when you are depressed and when communication breaks down with other people or yourself! Don't think we don't communicate with ourselves; we probably talk to ourselves more than we do to anyone else in our lives. We can make ourselves feel great or so badly.

We create our world through thoughts! So, quit blaming everyone else around us! Through meditation, we can change our thought processes. It does not matter what someone says or who they are. We are powerful beings who can change the way we think, how we feel; it has nothing to do with anyone else. It is all inside you, who you are! Remember, everyone has created and chosen the path they are on, the challenges and hurdles from which they are to learn! Facing challenges and hurdles is easy when we let God and the heavenly beings take care of the turmoil and problems around us.

Now, if you connect and focus the mind and body as one, there will no longer be trouble in your life? Right? Wrong! But problems will become minor (no longer Earth shattering). Things will become lighter and your health will be better. You will grow spiritually, physically and emotionally. You not only will become happier, but guess what? Those around you do too! You know why they can feel the lightness, the changing of your energy around you. You are no longer hiding; you are actually healing others around you wherever you go.

Focus on putting your mind and body in the same place at the same time.

Very relaxed, listen to yourself. Follow your instincts.

Spend some time by yourself each day, if only for a few minutes. You might open the door and find that you actually like yourself.

Loving or liking yourself are two of the most important things you can do. If you don't love yourself, how can you love others? You can't, it's very simple. You can pray all you want and you may think God doesn't hear, but he does. He's waiting for you to share His love for you by your loving yourself. Then, watch out. God's going to answer all of your prayers! So, watch what you're praying for; you just might get it!

Now, we're going to do some clearing and purifying of ourselves. We're going to get rid of the negativity and the darkness that surrounds us.

Remember, Shakespeare said "To thine own self be true". How scary! But think about how wonderful this could be!

Can you give 100% to yourself? Can you give 100% to work, family and friends? My answer is yes, absolutely! By giving 100% to yourself, it becomes so much easier to give 100% to others. You lose all judgments and expectations from others. You will become so much easier to give the 100% to others. You will become more receptive and understand them more fully.

However, you must first understand yourself, your actions and even your thoughts. Whenever, you start to say "I can't", you will change it to "I accept", or "I want to" or "It is simply this way". Change the thoughts from negative to positive! It only takes a moment.

You are taking control by controlling and changing your thoughts, and your perception of yourself and others. By doing this, you are taking control of who you are. You can rid yourself of negativity. Focus your positive energy by using meditation, reiki, chakra balancing, burning incense and lighting candles.

Rebecca's Metaphysical Moment

We don't have to be superstars to shine brightly.

CHAPTER TWELVE
Preparing For Life

August, 2005

When preparing for life, everything one can see may look great. Your home, for example, with all of the floors cleaned and crystal shining, surrounds you with beauty. That is until you open a closet, drawer or cabinet. Hidden away is all of the mess!

So, do we do the same thing with ourselves? There's the deep, dark and viscous part of our being which is a total wreck! Why? Because we are too busy preparing the outward appearance to look good. We do not take the time to clean up our inward self. We think if we hide it well enough, no one will ever know. Wrong! You know Spirit knows.

Most people are so shocked and horrified when they open that door that they immediately slam it shut and throw away the key, never wanting to re- enter one's mess or even to attempt to clean it up.

However, eventually, the mess will start sliding out into other areas, taking your perfect appearance with it and it will start interfering. Disease, illness, weight gain and unhealthy habits are just a few things we try to tuck back. So, then we have to go into that which has been closed away and really clean it up and purify it. It would be so much simpler to pick up and clean the little things, one at a time, avoiding the mess.

Now, we have to call in the cleaning crew of our God crew and Angelic realm. Now, it is time for a deep cleansing, a healing of the mind, body and spirit. When you heal one, a deeper cleansing will take place. It's like peeling an onion, one layer at a time. Sometimes the layers can be very thin, very fragile. We must go slow and easy in order to clean it all thoroughly, getting the inside sparking clean to match the outside.

So, where do you start, if you are going to start? Anywhere, any way you want. The most important thing is to start!

I recommend the first step to be meditation, getting in touch with yourself and God. Reconnect with the spirit that is inside all of us, our God source. Put down the phone, turn off the computer, television and all your other distractions; let all Earthly things go. Meditate for at least 15 minutes and feel the strength within your God Spirit. Step outside yourself while going into yourself, feel the oneness of yourself with God, your God!

The first and hardest thing to do is to have trust in yourself. Most people do not trust themselves. They have been told that they are unworthy of trusting themselves, and that they should only trust what man says. Wrong! Start cleaning the mess out by trusting in yourself. If your gut or God leads you, you will never go wrong! God will not lead you astray, but will show you the way!

Rebecca's Metaphysical Moment

Beauty is an illusion of the mind and a trick of the eyes. Beauty can be found in the heart for both have value.

CHAPTER THIRTEEN
The Perfect Diamond

October, 2005

Life is like a perfect diamond, one which has a slight flaw or imperfection. The experts see the flaw that lessens the value, forgetting about the true brilliance and beauty that outshines the flaw! We all can find flaws. Quit looking for flaws in things. Instead, look for the light and brilliance that surrounds the flaws! It still has tremendous value. It's still a beautiful diamond!

We all have flaws; but we still have tremendous beauty and value. So, don't sell yourself short because of a few flaws. We are not all twiggy models. For, perfection is how Spirit made us, no matter what! Flaws are an illusion. Everything is different; and everything is perfect in its own way. See yourself, and except yourself, as you are; A True Miracle Made in God's image.

The Bible says that many will come, but few are chosen. It tells us that we all have a choice. We choose whether we will be in another world, if we choose Heaven with God, or if we throw ourselves to evil and darkness. The choice is ours. What do you choose to do? Weigh odds and don't wait until you no longer have a choice. Why would you choose pain and suffering (hell) over Heaven? Darkness over light? Why follow in someone else's footstep and not create your own world and leave your own mark in life? Grains of sand form mountains! So, why can't you open such a small thing as the mind? Thinking for yourself is like looking into a mirror of knowledge. Open the mind's eye to see the whole of everything, not just a part.

You are a part of the whole realm of things. Heaven and Earth, man and animal, all spiritual beings that are among us. All things make up life. Open the consciousness to expand your reality, to expand your world, whether it is heaven or hell. The choice is yours. Do not follow the false prophets, closing your mind to all things. This is not living, only existing. Why waste a precious gift of life? Do not close your mind to choose.

This is not living as Spirit wants His children to live. There are many teachers in life! Death is the dying of the old ways. Rebirth is living in focus with Spirit through yourself and all things that surround us, making us healthy, whole and wise beyond our wildest dreams. We hold within us the seven candles of life, keeping our energies abundant and allowing us to feel the energies of the universe and Earth, taking us on a heavenly ride. You can do this by opening the mind's eye and heart, fulfilling your reality by changing your conscious being.

Light grows all things upon this Earth, all that has beauty and is heavenly! If you have pure intentions, then all things become pure! Your mind should be controlled by you, and only you! Man can take away everything that you have, but he cannot take your thoughts away! Spirit gave you your mind, not man. So, turn your brain around and communicate with Spirit. Open the right side of your brain and see how the left side starts sending different signals to the body and all things.

This is your gift from God, the Spirit-Maker. Man is the "spirit taker", taking away our spirit and filling our minds with greed, stress and sickness. Why? Because we know better; hence, illness is created for profit. When we are in touch within ourselves, we create good health and a loving connection to all things, as Spirit intended. You can heal yourself through changing of diet, your mind's choosing healthy abundance over illness, happiness over sadness.

There are 100 reasons not to do something, but all you need is one reason to do it and succeed, whether we want a successful marriage, business or wellness physically, emotionally and spiritually! We can do anything we want; all we need is one reason. The other 100 reasons to do it just don't count, they are forgotten the instant the one reason to do it enters the mind.

The choice is yours.

Rebecca's Metaphysical Moment

If the others come to seek you, where will you be?

CHAPTER FOURTEEN
Mars Nearing Earth

August 13,2003

On August 27, 2003, as I was originally writing this chapter, Mars reached its closest point to Earth in nearly 60,000 years. Much media attention was focused on this celestial event, however, something else greater was happening that did not receive the same attention but did occur; a shift in consciousness that is still happening today.

Standing in your light, you will see that the stars are just the stars. Now when I say this, yes, they do lead the way to heaven, but heaven is all around us. Earth is a heavenly body created to be so. We have been led to Heaven, to look upwards with our heads and not our hearts. By opening your heart, you can truly see God, the Supreme Being! You can feel heavenly; you will be surrounded by Heaven and God and the presence of all things which God provides. You will know the unknown. However, the shift of the consciousness within, takes a toll on some. The light will change from red to green, allowing us to see all things are possible. Not all things in the mind are good. Some literally will to crazy and some will choose to die, not understanding that the soul never dies. They will not have finished their lives here, but will abandon the Earth looking for resurrection! It will not come to those who go on uncompleted. If you do not open your heart to all things and all people, you then have given your life away. There will be no meaning in living when the heart cannot see, no understanding in life or life's purpose.

The greater the shift of consciousness, the brighter the light. You will illuminate and be a brother to and like the heavenly stars. You will feel the presence of God and the Angels. You will heal and feel at peace; you will see all things differently! You will speak and act differently. At that time, you well be able to take action. The action being that you will stand on your own two feet; becoming the teacher and the leader, the leader of your own life! By doing this, you are teaching others to look into their own hearts and feel the love that surrounds them.

You do not have to follow what someone else says is good or bad, only what your heart and inner self tells you. You can never be wrong; for, there is no wrong! Only learning lessons. Everything is as it should be by God's rules. Man is the one who sees Earth as hell and not a heavenly place to be. Why? Because man has made it a hell by not opening his heart, by not using a brilliant mind, by listening and believing someone else who is supposed to know, who is quote/unquote "leader", by not opening his consciousness and mind, by not listening to himself.

The world is in mass religious confusion at this time! Belief systems are dying. Why? Because we have not listened to God; we have listened to man! We cannot, I repeat, cannot grow until we open out hearts and let the shift of consciousness flow and lead us back to our God-like selves. In doing so, we enter a heavenly place here on Earth! Our troubles leave us; and love consumes us; a new and different love, understanding ourselves and others better, standing on solid ground, instead of constantly pulling ourselves out of the muck, or quicksand of everyday life! By making the changes in consciousness, the veil opens and we see the beauty in all things;

we see the inner light of God and our direct channels open. Earth and daily living then become heavenly!

So look within your hearts, open your mind to your inner self, and feel the warmth and love you feel for all things. God's love and presence will fill you, and then you won't need to look to the stars for Heaven. You will feel the Heaven we all have within each and every one of us. Then, you have allowed the consciousness to shift; and a great change will heal you. This change will heal you and those around you, making life wonderful instead of just bearable! A cleansing of the spirit will take place, a feeling of never being alone, never having fear, never doing what you are not supposed to do. For, you will see things differently; your manner of speaking will change, because your mind will change its thought process. At that time, you will feel safe! You will truly connect with God, the God within you. And guess what! All of these things are happening right now, here on this heavenly Earth, today, this moment! The choice is yours, my friend. God did not just create the Heavens and the Earth; he created an extension of Heaven on this place we call Earth!

Man is the one fouling up this Earth, not God. Man is the one leading us to think a certain way, be a certain way, not God. We live and dwell on God's playground! Do we act Godly? No. We pollute the air and water, we create wars unnecessarily. We destroy the land, our homes; and worst of all, we destroy our minds. All in the name of progress! Remember, we are all God's children, living on God's playground!

By shifting your consciousness, you can change all of the above. Look and you shall see. Look into yourself, and see a wonderful person. YOU!

Rebecca's Metaphysical Moment

Seek your freedom and strength from nature, it provides you all the things you need in this life.

CHAPTER FIFTEEN
The Power of All Creatures

September, 2011

Being very close to the Earth and Mother Nature, I draw much of my energy and strength from animals. You too, can do the same. Horses, for example, can give you peace and allow you to fly while staying grounded. In a sense, you meditate while riding, focusing the mind and body into one thing: teaching of a young horse. They make you feel truly free while you exercise your body. Freedom is a wonderful thing, to truly be in control of such a powerful beautiful creature, while leaving behind all the worries, stress and pressures of everyday life. You will be floating on a cloud while riding astride a beautiful being.

Horses depend solely on our care and attention. They each become attached to the one who cares for them. Having taught and trained horses for so many years has not only shown me what great, well-mannered and loving creatures they are, I have also learned more about love and to have no fear of anything. Horses allow you to go deeper inside yourself. They build your confidence and bring you forward to a different level of self-worth.

When working with animals, one mistake can cost you dearly, especially when dealing with large animals of such strength. You have to have both patience and knowledge, neither one comes overnight and process cannot be hurried. It takes time to develop and learn your training method.

I have many smaller animals on my ancestral land, including my beloved German Shepherds, who are trusting of all that I do. Loving and protecting, faithful and loyal to the end, they are soft and caring for all things in their lives. Not only their masters but also their young. They each have their own personalities and expressions, some sweet, some feisty and some hateful. Understanding the animal world helps me strengthen and understand the human world better.

Animals are such a strong symbol of freedom and love, but none more so than deer that roam the forests and grasslands. As fall approaches, their colors change from the spotted fawn to the more common darker and tannish gray, picking up the colors of the forest for protection. They truly are the most graceful of all of God's creation.

Rebecca's Metaphysical Moment

Whose laws are you following? Man's or God's?

CHAPTER SIXTEEN
The Laws

August 14,2003

The laws of the church are changing; however, the laws of Spirit have not changed in 10,000 years. God set the rules, sent us the mind and ability to act out our part in spiritual life. Man has been greedy and changed the laws from God's original plan. We are to be thinking human beings made in God's (Spirit) form. We have not listened to God, or our inner selves, rather to man's ego, being controlled and consumed by a power no greater than ourselves and certainly never as great as God or God's plan. God is the only one who can split the seas and walk on water. Man cannot, not unless it is God's will.

A loving spirit and a pure heart are the only things you need to elevate on up to a more heavenly serene place, a place where love is the flow. Forgiveness is freely given without penalties of a horrible life or death, for death is the reality of living, designed to show us we can live in harmony with the Earth and Earthly beings. God grants us this and all we wish for in life! God Spirit is the only one who should be in control of Earth and all things on Earth, not man! We were not put on this Earth to play follow-the- leader with a certain religion or a certain man. We were not put here to have our minds raped by someone who says that things are right or wrong! We were put here not to listen to man and not to fear God; through a man behind a pulpit, telling us to fear the unknown, to fear God. How wrong can this be?! Spirit is true to us and is a loving God. We can all see this if we open our minds and our hearts, if we connect to our true selves, to the God-being in each of us. HALLELUJAH!

God is alive and walks with us each and every day, protects us through the nights and leads us home at the end of our time and sending the Angels to help guide us. How wonderful! Man is the one who corrupts our lives and makes the laws to suit himself. "Play the game, or leave the table!" That is what man will tell you, not Spirit God!

God has given us the choice to stand in the light, not huddle in the fear and masses of men in the dark. Our lives should have clear meaning. Purity of thought and love should surround us. However, man says to love man and follow him; and his people use God as a fearful, powerful being that we will never see unless we follow all of man's laws! HOGWASH! What God thinks is to follow your heart, stay on your own path without being dragged along by the greedy and pious person. Be conscious of who you are, not who someone tells you that you are. When man tells you he expects you to do this or that, he is judging you. Only God can judge you, not man. Only God, the Supreme Being!

God created us, loves us and cares for our well-being. Remember, God is the true healer, not man. Our gift back to God is to trust and have faith in the spirit, to follow our own hearts and listen to our inner selves! By doing so, we are following God; for all he asks of us is for our love! He will provide the rest. Our lives will be bountiful and rich beyond any man who hoards his gold and silver. The veil is open, why not step through and see how heavenly Earth can be?

A new dimension surrounds us, yet we turn away and turn on the TV, to try to see what we call "the news of the day". The news of the day is: Follow your inner light and see where it may lead you. Where the news really matters is the new Dimension! Just don't let someone tell you that is the thing to do. Find out for yourself. By following God you will find the true leader in all things, someone who truly understands you will show you the way to love and the healing of yourself. A fleeting moment of sincere prayer is all it takes to find the true connection to God and His laws.

Let go of man's dictatorship description of right and wrong. Adhere to what the laws truly are and the way to live in harmony with all things on this

Earth and this universe. It's called the POWER OF GOD! He's calling; won't you answer?

The message has been delivered! The choice is yours alone. Not someone else's.

Rebecca's Metaphysical Moment

Enjoy this heavenly Earth and universe, filled with wonders and miracles of the stars. Most of all, stand on your mountain and enjoy being you.

CHAPTER SEVENTEEN
Energy Shifts

September 02, 2003

Today we are having many energy shifts. It is a time to awaken those who have been asleep, opening of the mind and the heart to stand on solid ground in God's presence, to truly open their eyes to all things which surround them on this palace we call Earth. It is a heavenly Earth that they will find which surrounds them and awaits them through looking and awakening the inner eye. They truly will see who they are, where they are going, and the whole of things; not only in this world, but in the next world also.

Completion is here; and we can feel God's presence and love through completion of ourselves, by opening the mind and heart, by seeing through the eye, by just enjoying who we truly are through our God source called Spirit!

So, let the rain and the true cleansing of all things begin through purity of the Earth and universe. They are both heavenly. Awaken your mind and body from the sleep you have been in. Enjoy the tomorrows through God's presence and the spirit of love.

Tear down the tabernacles of man and rebuild the faith given of all things through our Lord Jesus Christ. For, he is soon coming again to lead us truly home to the New Jerusalem. Wonders await us. Miracles are commonplace and you have just experienced one through Spirit. Hold forth your cup of faith no matter how small or empty. Soon, it will begin to overflow with wondrous possibilities for you; all through love and faith.

Don't forget to be thankful for all things in life, good or bad. Celebrate the lessons you learn. The courage is in another day. Have faith and tomorrow will come a beautiful day. As the seasons change, you will feel the change within and renewal of the body, mind and spirit. Remember, you are the holder of the seven candles inside you. Keep the flame burning brightly throughout all of time, for the spirit you carry never dies.

Rebecca's Metaphysical Moment

The Earth changes seasons like man changes clothes.

CHAPTER EIGHTEEN

Earth Changes: How It Affects the Changes in Your Life

October 16,2003

The seas are splitting and changing course like all things in life. Change is a natural occurrence, yet the one thing which humans are afraid of is change.

Some changes are good and some are not, but be assured change will happen. Blessings are presents; the not-so good changes are lessons. Learning from the lessons is a blessing. A growth experience is the ability to accept changes in our lives so that we can accept challenges and change the lessons. All things which God gives you are blessings. Open yourself and walk into the light of change, moving us forward and above all of those who are in a boat of pain.

Fulfill your life purpose here on this Heavenly Earth by opening your mind and heart, by accepting all that you are and all that you can be! A powerful person is capable of seeing change as a good thing, no matter how it appears to be, by creating your own castle and world. This is why we are called individuals. This is why we are not all alike. This is why God gave us minds and choices. What you do with your mind and the choices presented to you is up to you. You make it good or bad.

So, get out of the boat of pain and see yourself as a powerful individual. Make your choices with your head and your heart. Live in this Heavenly realm called Earth. Don't just be a cookie cutter person, following everyone else. Do your own thing without fear of being judged or being different, because guess what!? You are different from everyone else! That is why we are called individuals!

By becoming selfish, you become selfless.

By taking care of yourself and your choices, by standing by your decisions, it becomes easier for you to give and to help others freely without resenting it, or looking at this as a task to be done. Save time for yourself and spend quality time with others. You have to work by your time schedule, not that of others. We all have jobs to do. Create a happy space in which to work. Open your mind and free your heart by filling it with love. Have no regrets and learn the lessons. Count your many gifts and blessings daily.

First, thank God for who you are and ask who you want to become on this Earth and in this life. Work to become a truly free person, letting go of the stress and pressure of everyday life through the powerful person you truly are. Let go of mind-blockers, such as worry or judging others. They are only worms in the mind, taking up valuable space. Use that space for clearing, centering and listening to your heart and inner self which will tell you what you need to do. This helps you make clear and precise choices.

We all feel pain and loss in our lives. Pain lets you know that you are human. Remember this if you don't remember anything else, it will truly let you live. The choice is yours. Quit letting others make your choices. When you let go and are no longer a needy person, you will become more powerful, allowing understanding of all things and situations in your life to disintegrate and become less important. It will open and clear your path in life through God's eyes, not man's. Fear of living will disappear and your journey will become a wonderful adventure, guiding you forward toward a light of the unknown. For, all things in life are unknown. Do not question why; just accept the answers, your answers, your mind and your heart. Do not depend on others to give you their hearts; for not all humans can see. They are truly blinded by fear of the unknown and frozen in time and space. Take the first step and soon you will run freely, enjoying every moment of life which is exactly what we were intended to do on this heavenly Earth that God has created for us.

By doing the work, you get the rewards life has to offer us all. By receiving abundance and feeling worthy of abundance, you become abundant. By letting go, you actually are opening doors in your life that you never expected! Remember, God gave you life, so start living and feeling life. You now have truly healed yourself through God's love and through the love of yourself.

A realm full of possibilities is presented to us every day. Choose one and see where it takes you. The choice is yours. Your life belongs to no one but you. Sometimes, you have to close a door before you can open another. By closing the door on pain and suffering, you will open the door of love and peace; joy will come to your life and your life will become exciting. Close the door to challenge and open the door to success; you do this by making the right choices, centering and setting the stage for success, creating a wonderful world and filling your life with endless possibilities.

Don't worry about how you're going to do it, just do it! Use simple tools such as prayer, meditation, exercise and yoga, then soak in the tub or watch a gentle rain. How much easier can it be to get to simply being you, living life and playing upon this Earth? Be able to feel the joy and laughter that fills our hearts, healing ourselves and others through Spirit's love, the Supreme Being who made us in His image and connecting us to a higher purpose other than that of fear.

By showing kindness, we receive kindness. By showing love, we receive love. Laughter is infectious! Sing the psalms and let love's laughter carry through the universe, landing where it may and where it is most needed. Step out of the boat, close the doors and feel all of the things that life has to offer you. Start your engines for a better and healthier life; one that is meant for you because you are an individual. Enjoy! Your life is waiting!

Death sits on our doorsteps waiting, but by living and enjoying life we truly elude death. We trick death because we are truly alive and our souls never die, we just change clothes. We become another form of life. We simply go home for a while and live in God's space, evolving and changing our spirits and never truly leaving this world, just hovering over Earth in another space and time where there is no time; a space of conscious love, a space of healing and learning. We must earn the right to be there by accepting and knowing who we are here. God's love is unconditional; it has no limits. Man set the limits.

Count the stars and see yourself. For, we are all stars. We evolve on an Earthly plane and look above or around us for guidance. The true guidance comes from within us, from who we are and not what we are told to be by another human being. Their power and knowledge is no greater than our own God, who has the only great knowledge to share with us. He hears all of our thoughts, prayers and all that we speak. So, be careful what you think, pray for or speak. He is listening to you; and he will always answer. Even when you think he doesn't, he really does.

The only way for you to change your life and to grow, is by you! Your thoughts, your prayers, your speech; and all can be done by accepting yourself and your connection to Spirit. All you have to do is be willing to open and accept the changes you want to make, the changes within. Remember, the choice is yours. Look inside yourself for the answer and create a beautiful world, no matter what others see. You can see what is truly around you. We do truly live here on Earth in many different worlds. Some live in a world of poverty, some in a world of despair, and the list goes on. Why not make your world a world of light, peace, joy and laughter?

Humans, get out of the boat and be what and who you truly can be. By going inside, we heal the outside. We not only give of ourselves, but others come forward to give to you.

Rebecca's Metaphysical Moment

I am your heart; I am your mind. I am your vision; I am your light to follow through this life.

CHAPTER NINETEEN
The Arrival of Christ

(Channeled through the Angels: Blue, Gold, Red and Silver)
November, 2003

A falling star through the night brought the sound of Jesus' arrival, along with the animals lowing, sheep baaing and the lighting of the night like day.

Many a men came from afar, traveling over desert sand to become afraid and humbled in the presence of a small babe! Jesus has arrived from heaven, descended to Earth to experience birth, life and death; living and touching all people from infancy into manhood.

Wrapped in toweling, laying in a manager, so young yet touched the mind, body and spirit of grown men. At the time of His birth, the seas parted, throwing fishes into the nets of fishermen and a great feast began. Angels heard the chorus, sung and came to rejoice with men who brought the gold, frankincense, myrrh. Everyone and everything heard the rejoicing and knew that the true king among men had come, come to lead them to God's presence, love and compassion for all things, including themselves! Many a song, such as *"Hark! The Herald Angels Sing!"* has come from the minds of man, sent by the heavenly host on high.

It does not matter how or where you celebrate Christmas, so long as you celebrate it for the true birth of life. Christ was the first to rebirth and show the world on that wondrous night that all mankind is loved by God; that, by being touched by God and by the Godlike self!

Though each of us are human, we live in God's image; God lives in our hearts, mind, and spirits. All we have to do is take a look at the Christmas lights that surround us and remember that when a star fell, a whole new beginning took place. A new and wonderful world came alive with the arrival of the Christ child; new expectations, joy, love, and understanding of our fellow man. The heavenly host came by presenting us with such a special gift, a gift of love sent from Heaven above.

Amen! It brings us courage to carry on.

Here are a few Christmas ideas:

- Hang a candy can and give it to your favorite charity.
- Decorate the tree, giving love and healing to others as you do.
- Discover the true meaning of sharing by giving and receiving.
- Balance your holidays with passion, love, fun and good health.
- Ring in the New Year with true spirit.

Rebecca's Metaphysical Moment

Enjoy the hustle and bustle of the Holiday. During this time of
the year, watch the small Angels on this Earth.

CHAPTER TWENTY
The Light and Love of Christmas

November, 2003

Now is the time to look up towards the Heavens and feel the light and love from the universe and Spirit. By looking upwards and feeling the presence of God and the universal love, you are also feeling the gift of love within yourself. Warmth and love, not hate or anger and not grief or sorrow, is what makes the world keep turning. For, when you feel God's Supreme presence, you realize that you are never alone. Being alone is just a state of mind. Look around you, take a walk and feel the presence of nature, feel the presence of the Angelic realm, the wonders of the sun and stars. Feel the love and joy that surrounds you. Listen to the birds, the animals and the entire universe. Listen to the whispers in the wind. You are a holy creation, a gift from God's love, not a moment of passion. However, we should all feel passion about the things that surround us.

Stay grounded to this Earth, it lifts us towards our heavenly realm and takes us higher on our heavenly plane. Now is the time to journey on and reflect of Jesus, our Lord's life, to truly feel the love that God and Heaven brings. Enjoy the wonders of all of God's creatures to overcome our mind- state of being alone; to overcome being unaware of who we are and how we are connected to all things upon this Earth, and to feel joyful and abundant. Connect with your spirit self through the true feeling and knowledge of love. Be passionate about it. Be passionate about life. Lift yourself up to a higher plane of glory and revelation.

Mary traveled on a donkey to receive an unexpected gift of love made from a star of energy; Jesus, who arrived unexpectedly, bringing to this world hope, love and joy, standing on this ground to heal the afflicted and those in pain; healing the blind to see, the lame to walk, parting the waters and making us pure. How? By giving us knowledge through love, a gift of life he shared.

Now, share your gifts and receive the abundance and knowledge; receive from others the gift of love. Starting now, your life is waiting. Start this moment whole and new with love and heal not only yourself but those around you on this heavenly Earth. Feeling yourself heal, into greatness, you shall go by divine love and supreme healing. Healing through the master: Yourself.

The gift and connection are there, all you have to do is be ready and open to receive the gift of healing love through yourself. Let your God-self be touched by the supreme healing of God's love. Then, you too will have a rebirth through Christ and receive the ultimate gift of abundance. Merry Christmas to all of God's unique children.

Welcome to the healing power of one's self during the holiday season.

Love, God's Love.

Rebecca's Metaphysical Moment

Open your mind and your spirit to a realm of new possibilities, and opportunities for resurrection and rebirth.

CHAPTER TWENTY-ONE
Good Friday and Easter

March 25,2005

O h, great Spirit, I know I have been running on this heavenly Earth, trying to keep up with the masses of everyday Earthly life, trying to finish a job for which I feel unprepared, listening to men dooming themselves and all others, not listening to what God is saying nor living a life of good for all of mankind.

Good Friday, the day of miracles and dying, the crucifixion of our Lord Jesus, is when we celebrate the miracle of resurrection (rebirth) which we all have the opportunity to do. Through the crucifixion of Jesus, he cleansed us and also Himself. Through the resurrection or rebirth, He again became whole. He allowed not only himself, but all of mankind to live and to stop the anger, fear and fighting over a land that is not truly ours. This Earth, which God created for man, is a learning place. It is a place of love, not hate; a safe haven for man! Man was given the ability to think and control these own thoughts, however man has recreated a hell through destroying and controlling the thought process of others.

Well, God is tired of watching over His flock of non-believers, those who are unloving, always living fear and always listening to man but not to the God Almighty. He created us all for a purposeful life, not a life of being controlled by others, not a life of living in the box and always having fear of our most precious guardian; God! We hurry and hurry, but towards what? Do we even know? Do we ever stop and think about how wonderful it could be to heal ourselves and our lives? We are destroying our land, our water and our Earth. Why? Because we live in ignorance, listening to mankind and not to our God, the Supreme Creator of all.

That was not God's plan. That is why Jesus died, to help us understand that this Earth is a heavenly place and that there is no death, only a well-traveled path to a heavenly home or peace, light and love where we are reborn and

God still presides.

God is not an entity; He is the Supreme Being in spiritual form who knows ALL! Man does not know all, but stumbles around in the dark saying that he is superior, that he is knowledge, that he is just. No way can a man walk and talk in God's shoes. A man will get lost in God's footprints. Man does not rejoice Him, man fears retribution from Him. This is not to be. How can anyone fear such a loving and forgiving Supreme Being?

Angels are our guides and surround us all of the time, along with our past and family who have gone ahead of us. I know this is true. When man says you can't see Angels, I disagree, because I for one have seen the Angels. I for one have seen our loved ones who are helping to guard us. Open your minds and hearts, rejoice in life and live it to the fullest, because God is angry with the man who rejects him, sitting on the fence and can't see.

The tides will rise and come crashing down, the skies will open and cry in pain, gases will come and the Earth will open; all will consume man who is afraid, who hates and who does not believe in the rebirth. Buildings will fall, money will be gone and homes will disappear. Are you ready to love God? Are you ready to trust him? Are you ready to let God lead you to a more beautiful Earth where we will all be equal?

The antichrist is here and among us, but so are Jesus and His disciples, the Angels from above and God's presence. You only have to open your eyes and heart to truly see.

Don't let others tell you how to live or how to be. Just be yourself and see what a wonderful person you are. The rebirth is cleansing the body, mind and spirit, making you whole again to feel the love and joy of God.

The flowers will bloom again in the spring of life at any age, if you allow them. I am only one person, but it takes only one to part the waters of life and walk through to a new and better life upon this heavenly playground called Earth.

Love this Earth and universe. Dance upon it because it was freely given to us to protect, love and dance upon. It is our job to learn how to live here. Heaven is not that far away if you take off your shoes and feel it under your feet. Words and actions have destroyed man and Earth, not God. Pray and rejoice this day and this life. Stop committing the sin of evil destruction by greed, hate and fear.

The terrorists are here, yes. But what are we in a country, a world with no love? We terrorize ourselves into thinking the thoughts of man, letting evil cross our boarders, letting them in freely. Our economy is going to crash. We will no longer have the same existence. Our values will not be placed on monetary, but rather on survival and relying on God to provide for us. To come out of our boxes and help and love one another, not hate and not fear. For fear and anger have become our constant companions. You guard your crutch to stay in the box and in the dark to stay out of the light.

I tell you now to walk and work in harmony. Do not to be a martyr, live a truly free existence instead of only existing without a life.

I fear not, though I am tempted. I am lead to God to do His works in healing those I see, touch and love. Come today, the day of dying and rebirth, and join God and the Angelic realm by rededicating yourself to love and to God's wisdom of everlasting life. Wherever it might be, to learn the lessons of life, to truly learn God's laws and ways through connecting yourself with Him and working through Him. If not, all will be lost to you and your life will never have a true purpose. Only you as man can do it. I cannot do it for you, it is all up to you. Don't be a puppet on a string for man. Quit listening to the antichrist. Turn your intentions inward and listen to your God-self. Yes, terrorist and terror are here and they walk among us in many different forms, but survival is always on their minds because men of war are afraid of the hereafter. We can conquer them by showing our power, through standing in our belief that man cannot hurt us. God can save us! Amen!

Open your door to your neighbor, because they live in ignorance and in poverty of the mind. Let them see the shining of your light in your doorway where there stands an Angel, lighting, helping and healing those who come. The weapons of destruction then are dropped. We band together in that God will lead us to a plentiful land, a land of milk and honey and a land free of strife. Come, won't you today, and open your door of life?

I do not dictate the Bible. For, in many ways, it is true. I do not tell where or how to worship, only to keep in mind that man will try to lead you in the wrong direction sometimes. Decide which direction is right for you, through prayer and meditation you will never be wrong. You cannot stray from God when you truly open yourself and your heart to God. Who knows? You may see the Angel standing in your doorway. Speak to him and acknowledge him, for he is God's messenger to you on this planet called Earth, a home provided to you by God, a heavenly place to be. It's like awakening from a long nap. You will feel refreshed, calm and peace is with you. All then will be as it should be.

Rebecca's Metaphysical Moment

If you put your foot in the stirrup of life, you better be ready to ride.

CHAPTER TWENTY-TWO
Control and Greed

March 26, 2005

I have met mobsters and preachers. With some of them, I cannot tell the difference. Both are controlling and greedy. Most of mankind is! One will take your life by killing the body, the other by killing the spirit and mind! Is one any better than the other?

God has control of the mind, body and spirit. Why won't you turn yours over to Spirit? Do not judge, lest you be judged.

It's like driving a car. Once behind the wheel, you are in control and it's your job to stay on your side of the road. You have a 99% chance of having a wreck and injuring not only yourself, but others. Some may even die. Of course there is the other 1% chance that everything will be okay. Do you want to take that chance?

What I am saying is that it's okay to lose control, so long as Spirit is behind the wheel of life. Then, you can go anywhere-free, accident-free.

Does the road get bumpy? Yes. It may even have obstacles, detours and lots of turns. But with God behind the wheel to drive you, life will become easier and happier. The turns and bumps are no problem because you're flying on the Wings of Light.

Guess what! You can hope again, dream again and live life to the fullest again!

When man controls us, we take more and more drugs to feel better. We take a mood elevator to get up with, pills before meals for our stomachs and digestion, pills in the afternoon to get through the day, a drink or two after work to chill out. We even take a downer at bedtime to help us rest because we probably won't sleep after the day we've had. Life should not be this hard! Where's the cure? There is none. Depression sets in, we have mood swings and life's a bitch. You can't function at work, home or anywhere else. Man is telling you what to do and how to act. You start following others just like lambs led to the slaughter! Your health fails and your personal appearance is gone. You don't know who you are and you don't know where to turn.

Now is the time to heal yourself through love, light and healing, combining the mind, body and spirit through nothing more than getting in touch with who you are, your connections to God and Mother Earth, pulling your own strings of life and realizing that everything you have ever done has brought you to this place in life. You are a powerful being; a thinking, living individual who does not have to be like everyone else, who has the light of love in your hands and is never alone on this Earth.

Balance is the key here. Balance the energy systems (charkas) in the body, open the spirit self through meditation (another form of prayer) and keep the spirit alive and healthy. I call this a daily dose of Spirit-God, drink it in and feel the release; feel the love and joy. Look into the unknown and who knows what you might find! You may even find out that you like yourself, that you love your God, and that you feel better physically. You can think for yourself and make your own decisions!

Some will make excuses. Some will die and never know the joy of living! Don't be one of those with no soul to carry you forward, because YOU let someone steal it from you. Don't miss out on the joy of living, the joy of traveling, the joy of seeing, the joy of communication and power and of YOUR life.

Rebecca's Metaphysical Moment

Being guided by man is like reading a fable. Being guided by God
allows you to reach the stars.

CHAPTER TWENTY-THREE
The Country Clubs of Religions

October 22, 2011

The "church" was founded by Jesus Christ as a formal Earthly organization to establish a community of faith and love for all, as a gathering place and sharing their beliefs as a family. It was not founded to be an elite "country club"!

When a church has to approve a member, it's not right. When you have to take a copy of your tax return to the minister and his board before you can become a member, it's so wrong. If you are accepted into the congregation, then you are usually required to tithe, or give as they will tell you, up to 10% of your income, before you can partake in any official church activities. People have actually put up their homes and property in order to be accepted. Is this a loan you are getting from a church? Do you really want to join a church so badly that you sacrifice everything you have?

I know churches have to maintain upkeep on their buildings. They have utility bills, plus ministers have to be paid. However, how much do they really have to be paid? How much are they willing to take from others for their own personal gain?

I know of people who signed the contract, had personal financial loses and actually lost their homes to the church! The church not only took their property, but also dropped them from the church member registry! Literally kicked them out of the church and their homes! This is an act against God and religion!

I am not a religious person, as in organized religion. I am my own person and I am very spiritual! I was raised in the 'church family', but I never accepted all I was being told! I have never believed in fear! Why fear such a loving entity as God? Do you honestly believe God would not want your church to be loving and caring? Do you think God would want you to lose or give away your life to the 'church'! To Man!

Why should the church preacher, who is to be a prophet of God, live like a king? Wearing an expensive suit, handmade crocodile shoes or driving a new very expensive car, to belong to a church!

This is so wrong! Money will not buy your way into Heaven! All it will do is break you in this life and leave you with nothing but guilt!

I am not saying to not go to church. What I am saying is don't join a church to be socially accepted, that's when you are joining the "country club".

If a church does not accept you as you are and take what you are willing to give, then it's time to look somewhere else. Any church where you have to "wine and dine" the preacher before you are accepted, is ridiculous! This would be a country club that is judging you by race, gender, income and greed.

Also, if you cannot take communion before you pay or are approved, then go somewhere else. Did Christ require a "membership" of those he offered communion to? No! Think of when Christ fed, excluding no one, from the few fishes and loaves of bread that he gave freely.

When you join a church and listen intently to the teachings and sermons, you are getting their interpretation of the Bible; the word of the Supreme Being! You are told to live by what man is telling you, his interpretation of 'man's' laws, not God's!

Man tells you to fear God, to do the things man says, or you are hell bound! Bull! If you listen and open yourself to God, you will find that love and understanding of spirit will take you where you need to be, not man!

I know there are people who need religion and church in their life. I am not against all churches. I am against the churches who judge you before you ever join! Everybody wants to belong. Everyone looks for acceptance in their life.

I think it's wonderful to come together and rejoice in God's love. I cannot see a person going hungry, losing their homes or draining their bank accounts to fill the coffers with gold to one man!

I believe that if you choose to go to church, then give what you can and learn all that you can. Enjoy your part of a church family. You should have no worries when you are in a church home.

I am not against country clubs! It's a great place to socialize with friends and do the things that make you smile and laugh. With a country club, you know the cost upfront when you join and know that you have to be approved. Television evangelists are much worse than the "country club churches".

Give a donation of $10.00 and receive a blessing from them personally, along with a lovely book mark, personally blessed by them. For only $300.00, you might receive their audio book. This really gags me! If you want to be blessed, go within yourself and you will find that God has blessed you! You are blessed every day in this life, all you have to do is ask! Go within and look for your blessings. You should not have to pay anyone for a blessing!

Again I am not against churches and I am not against religion. I am against the false prophets who judge you and use fear to hold you captive. They use fear not love.

So many churches tell you that there are only a few Angels, this is wrong! There are thousands of Angels. When the churches limit the abilities of the Angels, they create a great divide between God and you.

I do not believe in a tollbooth religion to feed the preacher's coffers. This should not be!

Rebecca's Metaphysical Moment

Man can rise from the ashes of deceit and false information. Listen to your inner thoughts

CHAPTER TWENTY-FOUR
False Prophets

February,2005

By growing inside ourselves, we then start growing outside ourselves. Don't follow the false prophet!

There are many out there claiming to show you the way (the way through fear), and that God is this terrible wrath if you don't obey! Obey what? The laws of man or the laws of God? By opening your consciousness, your reality changes and God intervenes. Then, you will know what God wants of you. He asks nothing of you but your love in return for His gift of life, love and the mind. The rest is up to you. Spread the word through your light and healing energy! That's obeying God the Spirit, having trust in the unknown of God. Talking to the unknown of God is knowing God and fulfilling His requirements. Simply open your consciousness, which in turn will open your heart and lead you to a heavenly place here on Earth, loving all things and people, even yourself.

The false prophets are going to teach you how to become narrow in your thinking, leaving you in fear of the presence of God! His wrath, His judgment! How many men are you going to block your way in this life? Your mind? By using your mind, and gut the feeling of something is not right. Then it usually is not right! Listen to what is being told to you. Listen to what the false prophet is not saying. When you start listening, then the roadblocks disappear and our reality of seeing things differently takes us to a higher level of achievement in our own lives.

The Earth will not change until man changes his thinking, because thinking and the mind are the powers that keep man and the Earth from changing. Change your hell into heaven by changing your reality through thought. You are who you truly want to be, so be who you are. Touch your spirit and open your mind to all things around you, gathering what you need for completion. This then will make you a winner in all things. Only then will life become life as it was meant to be.

So, change your consciousness to expand your reality, to expand your world. Whether it be heavenly of hellish, the choice is the one you made, not some false prophet who is closing your mind to choices. This is not living as God wants His children to live. Death can be the dying of old ways, life is living in focus with God and the Spiritual Realm. All things that you have created make up a new and wonderful world filled with peace, love and joy from the heart! Your conscious reality has changed from darkness to light, from despair to a magical world filled with wonder. Darkness cannot grow, only light grows within the human soul. Light grows all things upon this Earth, all that is Heavenly. If your intentions are pure, then all things become pure. Heavenly voices on high, oh, how we feel their peace and love! Oh, how they rejoice when they feel your love, a love of purity from the heart. For, you have the true connection of mind, body and spirit. Enjoy the freedom of this life in peace upon this heavenly Earth.

Rebecca's Metaphysical Moment

Releasing the powers of an individual releases the freedom from within.

CHAPTER TWENTY-FIVE
Earth - The New Mecca

2009

In March of 2012, a friend called who also a channel, asking me to channel information for them. What I saw was that total devastation is coming, that something is re-entering the heavens and the Earth in a ball of hot fire! (Meteor Showers?). The food supply will be taken away for many. Cosmic upheaval and collapse will come. This will be the beginning of the New Earth, a cleansing all the Earth and its inhabitants. I saw what appeared to be that two stars will collide. Jupiter will erupt (or something of the sort), making this planet very hot, very desert like, especially in the western United States in the late summer months. Afterward, unusual weather in the mid- south will turn down the degrees in heat creating an autumn effect.

What you must remember, is the Earth (the world) keeps turning! A third of the United States along the east coast line including New York, Pennsylvania, New England, New Hampshire, Maryland and Washington, will be cleaned out by horrific water. East, east is the new mecca. Travel in those areas will stop! The power grids will hold for now but have to be changed.

This will happen over, and over again! The sands are shifting, the water is reclaiming the Earth as it once was and as it should be. Do not build your house on sand, it will be destroyed! This is bringing us back to the old ways. There will be less land, more water and survival of the fittest.

Vibrational energies will rise higher than they have ever been, going through the veil to help others quickly cross over by touching the hand of God and Jesus Christ, in a different, more personal way. While standing of this Earth, more and more people are seeing and being touched by Jesus, letting them know he is truly still alive.

A real test is coming around October 2013 (late 2013), when a giant storm (possibly a meteor storm) will close the grids down. More water will drown more of the land, pushing people literally to higher ground. This will be done so man can learn how to live together, share and get along with each other! Will there be fighting among the clans? Yes! However, because of the new energy opening, the clans will have to put aside their differences and work together, in order to survive, finding that a community of help is better than one of jealousy and bitterness of the heart. Judgment will still be made, however, it will be on a lower level and not tearing everyone's lives apart.

The snows and ice will be heavy in the United States, in the north, Midwest and upper east. Also, the Rockies will really be dumped on by heavy snow fall. The Earth needs nitrogen to replenish and nourish the soil. The core of the Earth is burning too hot, because of all the waste and chemicals that have been dumped and buried under the belly of the Earth.

Time is changing and ticking away! Make the most of each day!

www.ingramcontent.com/pod-product-compliance
Lightning Source LLC
Chambersburg PA
CBHW071012120626
46546CB00003B/1057